Mathematical methods

Unit Guide

The School Mathematics Project

CAMBRIDGE
UNIVERSITY PRESS

Main authors   Simon Baxter
                        Stan Dolan
                        Doug French
                        Andy Hall
                        Barrie Hunt
                        Lorna Lyons
                        Paul Roder
                        Jeff Searle
                        David Tall
                        Thelma Wilson

Project director   Stan Dolan

The authors would like to give special thanks to Ann White for her help in producing the trial edition and in preparing this book for publication.

Published by the Press Syndicate of the University of Cambridge
The Pitt Building, Trumpington Street, Cambridge CB2 1RP
40 West 20th Street, New York, NY 10011–4211, USA
10 Stamford Road, Oakleigh, Victoria 3166, Australia

© Cambridge University Press 1992

First published 1992

Produced by Gecko Limited, Bicester, Oxon.

Cover design by Iguana Creative Design

Printed in Great Britain at the University Press, Cambridge

British Library cataloguing in publication data

A catalogue record for this book is available from the British Library.

ISBN 0 521 40885 7

Contents

Introduction to 16–19 Mathematics

Nobody reads introductions and nobody reads teachers' guides, so what chance does the introduction to this Unit Guide have? The least we can do is to keep it short! We hope that you will find the discussion point and tasksheet commentaries and ideas on presentation and enrichment useful.

The School Mathematics Project was founded in 1961 with the purpose of improving the teaching of mathematics in schools by the provision of new course materials. SMP authors are experienced teachers and each new venture is tested by schools in a draft version before publication. Work on *16–19 Mathematics* started in 1986 and the pilot of the course has been used by over 30 schools since 1987.

Since its inception the SMP has always offered an 'after sales service' for teachers using its materials. If you have any comments on *16–19 Mathematics*, or would like advice on its use, please write to:

> 16–19 Mathematics
> The SMP Office
> The University
> Southampton SO9 5NH

Why 16–19 Mathematics?

A major problem in mathematics education is how to enable ordinary mortals to comprehend in a few years concepts which geniuses have taken centuries to develop. In theory, our view of how to pass on this body of knowledge effectively and pleasurably has changed considerably; but no great revolution in practice has been seen in sixth-form classrooms generally. We hope that in this course, the change in approach to mathematics teaching embodied in GCSE schemes will be carried forward. The principles applied in the course are appropriate to this aim.

- Students are actively involved in developing mathematical ideas.
- Premature abstraction and over-reliance on algorithms are avoided.
- Wherever possible, problems arise from, or at least relate to, everyday life.
- Appropriate use is made of modern technology such as graphic calculators and microcomputers.
- Misunderstandings are confronted and acted upon.

By applying these principles and presenting material in an attractive way, A level mathematics is made more accessible to students and more meaningful to them as individuals. The *16–19 Mathematics* course is flexible enough to provide for the whole range of students who obtain at least a grade C at GCSE.

Structure of the courses

The A and AS level courses have a core-plus-options structure. Details of the full range of possibilities, including A and AS level *Further Mathematics* courses, may be obtained from the Joint Matriculation Board, Manchester M15 6EU.

For the A level course *Mathematics (Pure with Applications)*, students must study eight core units and a further two optional units. The structure diagram below shows how the units are related to each other. Other optional units are presently being developed to give students an opportunity to study aspects of mathematics which are appropriate to their personal interests and enthusiasms.

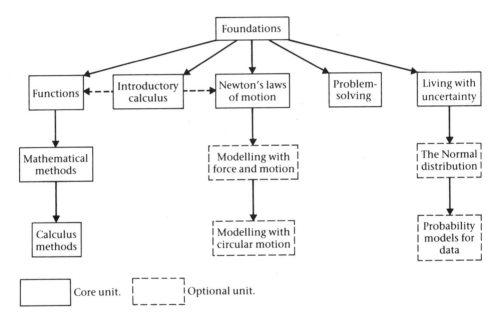

Core unit. Optional unit.

⟶ The *Foundations* unit should be started before or at the same time as any other core unit.

- - -➤ Any of the other units can be started at the same time as the *Foundations* unit. The second half of *Functions* requires prior coverage of *Introductory calculus*. *Newton's laws of motion* requires calculus notation which is covered in the initial chapters of *Introductory calculus*.

For the AS level *Mathematics (Pure with Applications)* course, students must study *Foundations, Introductory calculus* and *Functions*. Students must then study a further two applied units.

Material

The textbooks contain several new devices to aid an active style of learning.

- Topics are opened up through **group discussion points**, signalled in the text by the symbol

and enclosed in rectangular frames. These consist of pertinent questions to be discussed by students, with guidance and help from the teacher. Commentaries for discussion points are included in this unit guide.

- The text is also punctuated by **thinking points**, having the shape

and again containing questions. These should be dealt with by students without the aid of the teacher. In facing up to the challenge offered by the thinking points it is intended that students will achieve a deeper insight and understanding. A solution within the text confirms or modifies the student's response to each thinking point.

- At appropriate points in the text, students are referred to **tasksheets** which are placed at the end of the relevant chapter. A tasksheet usually consists of a self-contained piece of work which is used to investigate a concept prior to any formal exposition. In many cases, it takes up an idea raised in a discussion point, examining it in more detail and preparing the way for formal treatment. There are also **extension tasksheets** (labelled by an E), for higher attaining students, which investigate a topic in more depth and **supplementary tasksheets** (labelled by an S) which are intended to help students with a relatively weak background in a particular topic. Commentaries for all the tasksheets are included in this unit guide.

The aim of the **exercises** is to check full understanding of principles and give the student confidence through reinforcement of his or her understanding.

Graphic calculators/microcomputers are used throughout the course. In particular, much use is made of graph plotters. The use of videos and equipment for practical work is also recommended.

As well as the textbooks and unit guides, there is a *Teacher's resource file*. This file contains: review sheets which may be used for homework or tests; datasheets; technology datasheets which give help with using particular calculators or pieces of software; a programme of worksheets for more able students which would, in particular, help prepare them for the STEP examination.

Introduction to the unit (for the teacher)

Mathematical methods has been designed as a second-year unit for the *16–19 Mathematics* course. The main prerequisites are a knowledge of trigonometry, to include radians and trigonometric ratios for angles greater than 90°, and (for the later chapters) a familiarity with simple calculus. A prior study of the material in *Foundations*, *Introductory calculus* and *Functions* is therefore necessary.

Chapter 5 requires the use of a computer package to investigate differential equations. A number of such packages will plot a direction diagram for any given differential equation but the 'solution sketcher' program on the disc *Real functions and graphs* has the useful additional feature of allowing individual line-segments to be clicked together to obtain an approximation to the solution curve passing through a particular point.

Some additional notes on the individual chapters may prove helpful.

Chapter 1

Following a review of Pythagoras' theorem and its extension to three dimensions, several of its applications are introduced, including the equations of circles and spheres and the trigonometric identity $\sin^2 \theta + \cos^2 \theta = 1$. The solution of simple trigonometric equations is extended to the use of the phase-shifted sine wave, $r \sin (\theta + \alpha)$, as a replacement form for the linear combination of two waveforms, $a \sin \theta + b \cos \theta$. This leads to the addition formulas and double angle formulas. Finally, the sine and cosine rules are used to solve non-right-angled triangles.

Chapter 2

The vector equations of lines in two and three dimensions are developed, including methods of finding points of intersection. The angle between two vectors is found from the scalar product, which is also used to prove geometric results. The vector and Cartesian equations of planes follow and the role of the normal vector in finding angles between planes is demonstrated.

Chapter 3

The chapter opens by explaining how Pascal's triangle may be used in order to expand powers of $a + b$. For large powers a more general form is needed and so it is necessary to use the binomial theorem. The theorem is generalised to powers other than positive integers and the binomial series for $(1 + x)^n$ is developed and applied to small approximations. A consideration of inaccuracies in obtaining and recording data leads to a study of how errors and relative errors are affected by arithmetical operations.

Chapter 4

Starting with a revision of the idea of functions of functions, this chapter leads to the chain rule and enables students to extend differentiation results from simple functions to composite functions. This technique is applied to inverse functions and to x^n for negative and fractional n.

Chapter 5

The final chapter of the unit extends students' ideas of integration to differential equations. These are mainly tackled numerically although some comparison between numerical and analytical methods is made. Some use is made of the SMP gradient measurer and a line-segment plotting/solution sketching program is essential. Students may find the copymaster *Differential equations* in the CASIO *fx–7000GA* pack helpful. The last section on the formulation and solution of differential equations is a challenging one, the choice of method of solution being left open to the student.

Tasksheets and resources

This list gives an overview of where tasksheets are to be used. Items in *italics* refer to resources not included in the main text.

- The software *Real functions and graphs* and SMP gradient measurers may be ordered from Cambridge University Press.

- The multicubes may be ordered from an educational supplier.

- The other italicised items can be found in the second pack for the *Teacher's resource file.*

1 The power of Pythagoras

1.3 Trigonometric identities

> (a) How does the diagram above show that $\sin^2 \theta + \cos^2 \theta = 1$?
>
> (b) Does this result hold for **any** value of θ?
>
> (c) Explain why $\tan \theta = \dfrac{\sin \theta}{\cos \theta}$.
>
> (d) If $\sin \theta = \frac{1}{3}$, what is the value of (i) $\cos \theta$ (ii) $\tan \theta$?

(a) By Pythagoras, $\sin^2 \theta + \cos^2 \theta = 1$.

(b) Since the lengths of the sides of the triangle will be $|\sin \theta|$ and $|\cos \theta|$ for any value of θ, the identity will hold.

(c) For angles of less than $90°$, $\tan \theta$ is defined as $\dfrac{\text{opposite}}{\text{adjacent}}$.

For general angles, $\tan \theta$ is defined to be $\dfrac{\sin \theta}{\cos \theta}$. (See *Functions*, chapter 2.)

(d) (i) Since $\cos^2 \theta = 1 - \sin^2 \theta$,

$$\cos \theta = \sqrt{\left(1 - \frac{1}{9}\right)} = \frac{2\sqrt{2}}{3}$$

(ii) Using $\tan \theta = \dfrac{\sin \theta}{\cos \theta}$,

$$\tan \theta = \frac{1}{3} \div \frac{2\sqrt{2}}{3} = \frac{1}{2\sqrt{2}}$$

1.4 $r\sin(\theta + \alpha)$

Explain why

$$2.5 \sin \theta + 1.5 \cos \theta \leqslant 2$$

if the wardrobe is to go through the doorway.

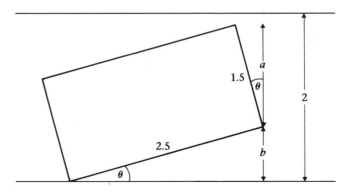

From the diagram,
$a = 1.5 \cos \theta$
$b = 2.5 \sin \theta$
So, if the wardrobe is to pass through the doorway,
$a + b \leqslant 2$
$\Rightarrow 1.5 \cos \theta + 2.5 \sin \theta \leqslant 2$

1.5 Addition formulas

(a) Use the diagram to explain why
$\sin (A + B) = a \sin A + b \cos A$. Hence obtain the expansion

$$\sin (A + B) = \sin A \cos B + \cos A \sin B$$

(b) Similarly, explain why $\cos (A + B) = a \cos A - b \sin A$.
Hence show that

$$\cos (A + B) = \cos A \cos B - \sin A \sin B$$

(c) Use your answers to (a) and (b) to help you obtain
expressions for $\sin 2A$ and $\cos 2A$.

(d) Check the identities you have obtained by substituting
various values for A and B.

(a)

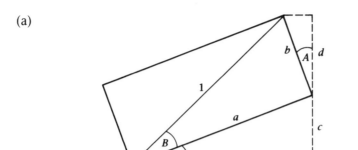

$$c + d = 1 \sin (A + B)$$
$$\text{also, } c + d = a \sin A + b \cos A$$
$$\Rightarrow \ \sin (A + B) = a \sin A + b \cos A$$

$$\text{Then } a = \cos B, \quad b = \sin B$$
$$\Rightarrow \ \sin (A + B) = \sin A \cos B + \cos A \sin B$$

(b)

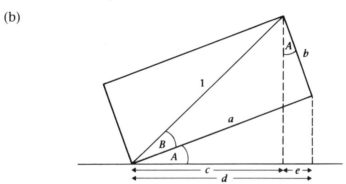

From the diagram, $c = d - e$
$$d = a \cos A, \quad e = b \sin A$$
$$c = 1 \cos (A + B)$$
$$\Rightarrow \ \cos (A + B) = a \cos A - b \sin A$$
$$\Rightarrow \ \cos (A + B) = \cos A \cos B - \sin A \sin B$$

(c)   (i)   In $\sin (A + B) = \sin A \cos B + \cos A \sin B$, let $B = A$
Then $\sin 2A \ = \sin A \cos A + \cos A \sin A$
$$= 2 \sin A \cos A$$

(ii)   In $\cos (A + B) = \cos A \cos B - \sin A \sin B$, let $B = A$
Then $\cos 2A = \cos A \cos A - \sin A \sin A = \cos^2 A - \sin^2 A$
The identity $\cos^2 A + \sin^2 A = 1$ can be used to obtain two
alternative expressions for $\cos 2A$:
$$\cos 2A = 1 - 2 \sin^2 A$$
and $\cos 2A = 2 \cos^2 A - 1$

(d) Checks are straightforward to make. For example,
$$\sin (25° + 35°) = \sin 60° = 0.866$$
$$\sin 25° \cos 35° + \cos 25° \sin 35° = 0.423 \times 0.819 + 0.906 \times 0.574$$
$$= 0.866$$

3

1.6 Solution of non-right-angled triangles: the cosine rule

Do you think that the journalist was right to say that the liner *Archimedes* ignored the signal or is it possible that they were unable to hear it? (Consider an accurate plan of the course taken by the vessels.)

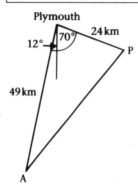

From the diagram it is clear that the distance between the two boats is approximately 50 km, the limit of the radio range.

The exact distance can be found either by drawing (which has limited accuracy) or by calculation, in which case we need an appropriate method.

1.7 Solution of non-right-angled triangles: the sine rule

By drawing a diagram for the triangle, show that this is not the only solution for angle *B*.

How many solutions are possible? What are they?

A sketch of the triangle shows **two** possible positions for B, corresponding to the two solutions.

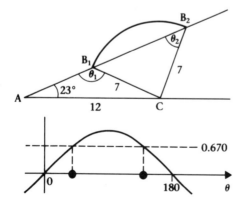

This is sometimes called the 'ambiguous case' of the sine rule.

There are many angles which have sine equal to 0.670. Two of these angles are in the range $0° < \theta < 180°$.

From the graph, θ could be either 42.1° or $180° - 42.1° = 137.9°$.

Pythagoras' theorem

1

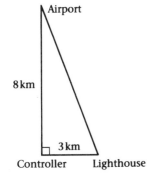

Using Pythagoras' theorem, the controllers can calculate the distance from the lighthouse to the airport as

$$\sqrt{(8^2 + 3^2)} = \sqrt{73}\,\text{km}$$

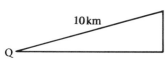

They can then find the distance of the plane from the airport, again using Pythagoras' theorem, as

$$\sqrt{(73 + 1)} = \sqrt{74} \approx 8.6\,\text{km}$$

Since this is less than 10 km the pilot should have sufficient fuel.
In fact, if the plane lands at Q, the distance from the lighthouse could be as much as

$$\sqrt{(100 - 1)} = \sqrt{99} \approx 9.95\,\text{km}$$

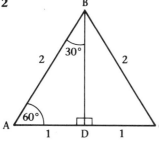

He would therefore have flown a further 1.35 km.

2

By Pythagoras' theorem, $BD^2 = 4 - 1 = 3$

i.e. $BC = \sqrt{3}$

You can then read off the required trigonometric ratios.

	30°	60°
sin	$\dfrac{1}{2}$	$\dfrac{\sqrt{3}}{2}$
cos	$\dfrac{\sqrt{3}}{2}$	$\dfrac{1}{2}$
tan	$\dfrac{1}{\sqrt{3}}$	$\sqrt{3}$

5

3

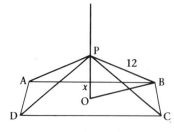

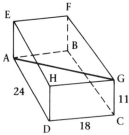

Let the flagpole be supported at the point P, a distance x m from its base O.
By Pythagoras, $x^2 = 12^2 - OB^2$

By considering the base, $OB^2 = 2.5^2 + 4^2$
$$= 22.25$$
$\Rightarrow x^2 = 144 - 22.25 = 121.75$
$\Rightarrow x = 11.034$
The height of the flagpole ≈ 22.1 m

4 (a)

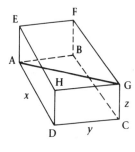

The diagonal AG is the hypotenuse of the right-angled triangle AGC
i.e. $AG^2 = AC^2 + CG^2$
AC is the hypotenuse of the right-angled triangle ADC
i.e. $AC^2 = AD^2 + CD^2$
$\Rightarrow AC = 30$
and $AG = \sqrt{(900 + 121)} = 31.95$ cm

(b) Generalising this result, if $AD = x$, $CD = y$, $CG = z$
then $AC^2 = x^2 + y^2$
so $AG^2 = AC^2 + CG^2$
$$= (x^2 + y^2) + z^2$$
$$= x^2 + y^2 + z^2$$
$\Rightarrow AG = \sqrt{(x^2 + y^2 + z^2)}$

5 By 'trial and error' you can find

3	4	5		5	12	13	8	15	17	7	24	25	20	21	29
6	8	10		10	24	26						
9	12	15										
12	16	20										
15	20	25										

Circles and spheres

TASKSHEET

COMMENTARY

2

1 (a)

If a point lies on the circle, its coordinates will satisfy the equation $x^2 + y^2 = 25$.

Thus, since $4^2 + 3^2 = 25$, the point $(4, 3)$ lies on the circle.

Further points which lie on the circle are $(-3, 4)$ and $(-5, 0)$.

(b) From the argument above, the equation of the circle is $x^2 + y^2 = 25$.

2 (a)

If the point P lies on the circle, then $CQ^2 + PQ^2 = 25^2$.

All the given points satisfy this equation.

(b) Since $CQ = x - 2$ and $PQ = y - 5$, the equation of the circle is $(x - 2)^2 + (y - 5)^2 = 25^2$.

3

$(x - a)^2 + (y - b)^2 = r^2$ represents a circle, centre (a, b), radius r.

4 (a)

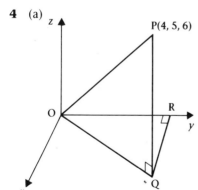

If Q is the foot of the perpendicular from P to the x–y plane, then PQ has length 6.

So, applying Pythagoras to triangle OPQ,

$$OP^2 = PQ^2 + OQ^2 = 6^2 + OQ^2$$

You can find OQ by applying Pythagoras to triangle ORQ.

$OR = 5, RQ = 4 \Rightarrow OQ^2 = 5^2 + 4^2$

Thus $OP^2 = 6^2 + 5^2 + 4^2 = 77 \Rightarrow OP \approx 8.77$

You can use a similar method to give:

(b) 5   (c) 5   (d) $\sqrt{14} \approx 3.74$

5 (a) 3   (b) 2   (c) 4

$$PQ^2 = 3^2 + 2^2 + 4^2 = 29$$
$$\text{So } PQ = \sqrt{29} \approx 5.39$$

6 Using the method of question 5,

(a) $PQ^2 = 3^2 + 1^2 + 6^2 = 46 \Rightarrow PQ = \sqrt{46} \approx 6.78$

(b) $PQ^2 = 4^2 + 11^2 + 1^2 = 138 \Rightarrow PQ = \sqrt{138} \approx 11.75$

(c) $PQ = \sqrt{[(x - a)^2 + (y - b)^2 + (z - c)^2]}$

7 (a) $OP = \sqrt{(x^2 + y^2 + z^2)}$

Since $OP = r$, the equation of the sphere is

$$\sqrt{(x^2 + y^2 + z^2)} = r$$

This is more usually written as $x^2 + y^2 + z^2 = r^2$.

(b) If the centre is at (a, b, c), the distance of a point on the sphere from (a, b, c) is

$$\sqrt{[(x - a)^2 + (y - b)^2 + (z - c)^2]}$$

Hence the equation is

$$\sqrt{[(x - a)^2 + (y - b)^2 + (z - c)^2]} = r$$
$$\text{or} \qquad (x - a)^2 + (y - b)^2 + (z - c)^2 = r^2$$

a sin θ + *b* cos θ

1 (a)

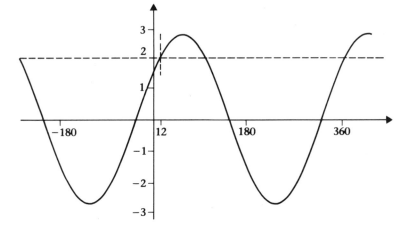

(b) The approximate solution is 10°. [The value predicted by theory is 12.4°.]

(c) (i) The greatest height above ground is 2.9 m, which occurs at an angle of approximately 60° (59° in theory).

   (ii) The wardrobe may be tipped at any angle between 0° and 12°.

2 (a)

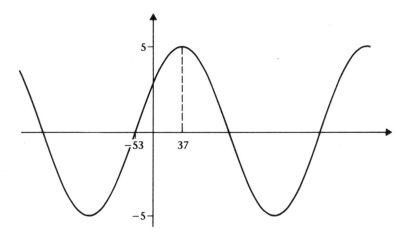

The graph is a phase-shifted sine wave.

(b) $y = 5 \sin (x + 53°)$ since the graph has amplitude 5 and is $y = 5 \sin x$ translated through $\begin{bmatrix} -53 \\ 0 \end{bmatrix}$.

(c) –

3

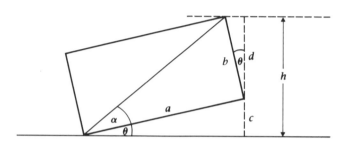

(a) (i) $h = c + d = a \sin \theta + b \cos \theta$

(ii) $\dfrac{h}{r} = \sin (\theta + \alpha) \Rightarrow h = r \sin (\theta + \alpha)$

(b) $r^2 = a^2 + b^2$ and $\tan \alpha = \dfrac{b}{a}$

Thus, you can write $a \sin \theta + b \cos \theta$ in the form $r \sin (\theta + \alpha)$, where $r^2 = a^2 + b^2$ and $\tan \alpha = \dfrac{b}{a}$.

4 (a) $r = \surd(4^2 + 7^2) = 8.06$

$\tan \alpha = \dfrac{7}{4} \Rightarrow \alpha = 60.3°$

$\Rightarrow 4 \sin \theta + 7 \cos \theta = 8.06 \sin (\theta + 60.3°)$

(b) –

Extending the method

4E

1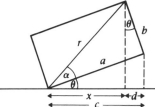

(a) (i) $x = r \cos(\theta + \alpha)$

(ii) $x = c - d = a \cos \theta - b \sin \theta$

(b) $a \cos \theta - b \sin \theta = r \cos(\theta + \alpha)$

2 $y = c - d$
   $= a \sin \theta - b \cos \theta$
Also $y = r \sin(\theta - \alpha)$
$\Rightarrow a \sin \theta - b \cos \theta = r \sin(\theta - \alpha)$

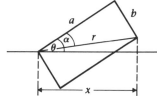

3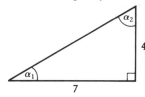

Considering the projections on the x-axis
$x = a \cos \theta + b \sin \theta$
Also $x = r \cos(\theta - \alpha)$
$\Rightarrow a \cos \theta + b \sin \theta = r \cos(\theta - \alpha)$

4 (a) $r_1 = \sqrt{(49 + 16)} = \sqrt{65}$ $\alpha_1 = \tan^{-1} \dfrac{4}{7} = 29.7°$

(b) $r_2 = \sqrt{(16 + 49)} = \sqrt{65}$ $\alpha_2 = \tan^{-1} \dfrac{7}{4} = 60.3°$

(c) You can consider the function either as a sine graph with a phase shift of $-29.7°$ or as a cosine graph of phase shift $+60.3°$.

(d) $\alpha_1 + \alpha_2 = 90°$. This relationship may be seen clearly from the triangle

$$\alpha_2 \quad 4 \quad \alpha_1 \quad 7$$

5 (a) $25 \cos(\theta - 73.7°)$ (b) $13 \sin(\theta + 22.6°)$

(c) $41 \sin(\theta - 77.3°)$ (d) $4.47 \sin(\theta + 30°)$

6 (a) $3 \sin\left(\theta + \dfrac{\pi}{6}\right)$ (b) $3 \cos\left(\theta - \dfrac{\pi}{3}\right)$

(c) $3 \sin\left(\theta + \dfrac{11\pi}{6}\right)$ (d) $3 \cos\left(\theta + \dfrac{5\pi}{3}\right)$

The cosine rule

1 $h = b \sin A$
$y = b \cos A$

2 $x = c - y$, because $x + y = c$
$x = c - b \cos A$

3 $a^2 = h^2 + x^2$
$\quad = (b \sin A)^2 + (c - b \cos A)^2$

4 $a^2 = b^2 \sin^2 A + c^2 - 2bc \cos A + b^2 \cos^2 A$
$\quad = b^2 + c^2 - 2bc \cos A$, since $\cos^2 A + \sin^2 A = 1$

Cosine rule:

$$a^2 = b^2 + c^2 - 2bc \cos A$$

5 If $A = 90°$, $\cos A = 0$ and the cosine rule gives $a^2 = b^2 + c^2$, which is Pythagoras' theorem.

If $A < 90°$, $a^2 < b^2 + c^2$, which corresponds with the result given by the cosine rule.

6 (a) $c^2 = a^2 + b^2 - 2ab \cos C$

(b) $b^2 = a^2 + c^2 - 2ac \cos B$

7 The result also applies to obtuse-angled triangles. The proof can easily be modified to show this.

If $90° < A < 180°$, $a^2 > b^2 + c^2$, which corresponds with the result given by the cosine rule, since $\cos A$ is negative when A is obtuse.

The sine rule

1 $h_1 = c \sin A$
$\frac{1}{2} bh_1 = \frac{1}{2} bc \sin A$

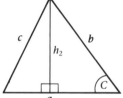

Note: This is a more useful expression for the area of a triangle than $\frac{1}{2}bh_1$, since it is given in terms of sides and angles.

> Area of triangle $= \frac{1}{2} bc \sin A$
> $= \frac{1}{2} \times$ product of two sides $\times$ sine of included angle.

2

$h_2 = b \sin C$
Area $= \frac{1}{2}ab \sin C$

3 $\frac{1}{2}bc \sin A = \frac{1}{2}ab \sin C$
$\Rightarrow c \sin A = a \sin C$
$\Rightarrow \dfrac{a}{\sin A} = \dfrac{c}{\sin C}$

4 By symmetry, if c is the base, area $= \frac{1}{2}ac \sin B$

5 $\frac{1}{2}ac \sin B = \frac{1}{2}bc \sin A$
$\Rightarrow \dfrac{a}{\sin A} = \dfrac{b}{\sin B}$

So, combining this result with that obtained in question 3, gives

> Sine rule:
> $$\dfrac{a}{\sin A} = \dfrac{b}{\sin B} = \dfrac{c}{\sin C}$$

6 Area $= \frac{1}{2} \times 4 \times 7 \times \sin 30° = 7\,\text{cm}^2$

2 Vector geometry

2.1 Vectors and position vectors

(a) What are the position vectors of the aircraft A and B one minute after A takes off?

(b) How are the vectors $\overrightarrow{OA}, \overrightarrow{OB}, \overrightarrow{AB}$ related?

(c) What are the components of the vector $\overrightarrow{AB}$?

(d) What information does the vector $\overrightarrow{AB}$ give?

(a) Taking the vector $\begin{bmatrix} a \\ b \\ c \end{bmatrix}$ to represent a position a km east, b km

north and c km high, relative to the point O, aircraft A has

position vector $\overrightarrow{OA} = \begin{bmatrix} 1 \\ 5 \\ 0.8 \end{bmatrix}$ and B has position vector $\overrightarrow{OB} = \begin{bmatrix} 5 \\ 5 \\ 4 \end{bmatrix}$.

(b), (c) $\overrightarrow{OA} + \overrightarrow{AB} = \overrightarrow{OB}$ **or** $\overrightarrow{AB} = \overrightarrow{OB} - \overrightarrow{OA} = \begin{bmatrix} 4 \\ 0 \\ 3.2 \end{bmatrix}$

(d) The vector $\overrightarrow{AB}$ represents the **displacement** from A to B i.e. it gives the distance and direction of B from A.
NB. $\overrightarrow{AB}$, unlike $\overrightarrow{OA}$ and $\overrightarrow{OB}$, is not a position vector since it is not related to any origin.

2.2 Equations of lines

(a) In what direction is aircraft B flying?

(b) Find the vector $\overrightarrow{AB}$ at intervals of 1 minute.

(c) What do you notice?

(d) How could the vector $\begin{bmatrix} 0 \\ 5 \\ 0 \end{bmatrix}$ in the equation for B be modified to avoid calamity?

(a) B is flying in the direction of the vector $\begin{bmatrix} 0 \\ 5 \\ 0 \end{bmatrix}$.

(b)

t	0	1	2	3	4	5
$\overrightarrow{OA}$	$\begin{bmatrix} 0 \\ 0 \\ 0 \end{bmatrix}$	$\begin{bmatrix} 1 \\ 5 \\ 0.8 \end{bmatrix}$	$\begin{bmatrix} 2 \\ 10 \\ 1.6 \end{bmatrix}$	$\begin{bmatrix} 3 \\ 15 \\ 2.4 \end{bmatrix}$	$\begin{bmatrix} 4 \\ 20 \\ 3.2 \end{bmatrix}$	$\begin{bmatrix} 5 \\ 25 \\ 4.0 \end{bmatrix}$
$\overrightarrow{OB}$	$\begin{bmatrix} 5 \\ 0 \\ 4 \end{bmatrix}$	$\begin{bmatrix} 5 \\ 5 \\ 4 \end{bmatrix}$	$\begin{bmatrix} 5 \\ 10 \\ 4 \end{bmatrix}$	$\begin{bmatrix} 5 \\ 15 \\ 4 \end{bmatrix}$	$\begin{bmatrix} 5 \\ 20 \\ 4 \end{bmatrix}$	$\begin{bmatrix} 5 \\ 25 \\ 4 \end{bmatrix}$
$\overrightarrow{AB}$	$\begin{bmatrix} 5 \\ 0 \\ 4 \end{bmatrix}$	$\begin{bmatrix} 4 \\ 0 \\ 3.2 \end{bmatrix}$	$\begin{bmatrix} 3 \\ 0 \\ 2.4 \end{bmatrix}$	$\begin{bmatrix} 2 \\ 0 \\ 1.6 \end{bmatrix}$	$\begin{bmatrix} 1 \\ 0 \\ 0.8 \end{bmatrix}$	$\begin{bmatrix} 0 \\ 0 \\ 0 \end{bmatrix}$

(c) The aircraft would collide after 5 minutes.

(d) Assuming that aircraft B wishes to maintain the same course, i.e. due east, it would achieve this by altering the *y*-coordinate of its velocity, for example to 6.

2.3 Scalar products

$$\mathbf{a} = \begin{bmatrix} 3 \\ 1 \end{bmatrix} \qquad \mathbf{b} = \begin{bmatrix} 2 \\ 3 \end{bmatrix}$$

How could you find the angle, θ, between the two vectors?

One way of finding the angle would be to use the cosine rule on triangle OAB. The lengths OA and OB can be found using Pythagoras' theorem and since $\overrightarrow{AB} = \overrightarrow{OB} - \overrightarrow{OA}$ its length can also be found.

$OA = \sqrt{(3^2 + 1^2)} = \sqrt{10} \qquad OB = \sqrt{(2^2 + 3^2)} = \sqrt{13}$

$\overrightarrow{AB} = \mathbf{b} - \mathbf{a} = \begin{bmatrix} -1 \\ 2 \end{bmatrix} \qquad AB = \sqrt{(1^2 + 2^2)} = \sqrt{5}$

So, by the cosine rule $AB^2 = OA^2 + OB^2 - 2\,OA\,OB\cos\theta$

$\Rightarrow \qquad 5 = 10 + 13 - 2\sqrt{10}\sqrt{13}\cos\theta$

$\Rightarrow \cos\theta = \dfrac{9}{\sqrt{130}} = 0.7894 \quad \Rightarrow \quad \theta = 37.9°$

2.4 Properties of the scalar product

> What can you say about two vectors **a** and **b** if **a** . **b** = 0?

If **a** . **b** = 0 then $ab \cos \theta = 0$

so **either** a or $b = 0$ (in which case at least one of the vectors is a zero vector)

or $\cos \theta = 0$ i.e. $\theta = 90°$ and **a** is perpendicular to **b**.

2.5 Vector equations of planes

> (a) What are the vectors $\overrightarrow{AB}$ and $\overrightarrow{AC}$?
>
> (b) Where are the points with the following position vectors?
>
>   (i) $\overrightarrow{OA} + \tfrac{1}{2}\overrightarrow{AB} + \tfrac{1}{2}\overrightarrow{AC}$
>
>   (ii) $\overrightarrow{OA} + \tfrac{1}{4}\overrightarrow{AB} + \tfrac{1}{4}\overrightarrow{AC}$
>
>   (iii) $\overrightarrow{OA} + 2\overrightarrow{AB} - \overrightarrow{AC}$
>
>   (iv) $\overrightarrow{OA} + \lambda\overrightarrow{AB} + \mu\overrightarrow{AC}$
>
> (c) Can **every** point in the plane ABC be found from a suitable choice of λ and μ in (b)(iv)?

(a) $\overrightarrow{AB} = \mathbf{b} - \mathbf{a} = \begin{bmatrix} -3 \\ 5 \\ 0 \end{bmatrix}$ $\overrightarrow{AC} = \mathbf{c} - \mathbf{a} = \begin{bmatrix} -3 \\ 0 \\ 4 \end{bmatrix}$

(b) (i) M, the midpoint of BC.

    (ii) D, the midpoint of AM.

    (iii) $\overrightarrow{OA} + 2\overrightarrow{AB} - \overrightarrow{AC}$ is the point F in the plane ABC, where $\overrightarrow{AE} = 2\overrightarrow{AB}$ and $\overrightarrow{EF} = \overrightarrow{AC}$.

    (iv) $\overrightarrow{OA} + \lambda\overrightarrow{AB} + \mu\overrightarrow{AC}$ is a general point in the plane ABC.

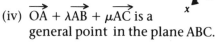

(c) Every point in the plane ABC can be reached by the vector $\overrightarrow{OA}$ together with some combination of vectors $\overrightarrow{AB}$ and $\overrightarrow{AC}$.

2.6 Cartesian equation of a plane

(1, 3, 0) is a point which satisfies the equation $x + y + z = 4$.
Find other points which satisfy this equation and consider
their positions in space. What does the equation represent?

Some obvious points include (4, 0, 0),   (0, 4, 0),   (0, 0, 4),   (3, 1, 0),
(2, 2, 0) etc. If these are plotted, the following diagram is obtained:

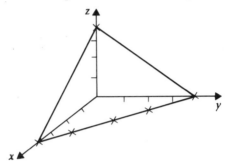

This suggests that $x + y + z = 4$ represents a plane.

2.7 Finding angles

(a) When two planes intersect, which angle is considered to be
the angle between the planes?

(b) How can this angle be calculated given the Cartesian
equations of the planes?

(a)

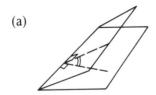

It is conventional to consider the angle
between two planes to be the angle
formed by the two perpendiculars to the
line of intersection of the plane.

(b)

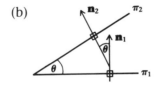

Since it is the **normals** that specify the
direction between the planes, the angle
between the planes can be found from the
angle between the two normals.

Vectors and position vectors

1 (a)

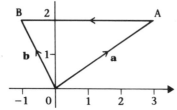

$$\overrightarrow{AB} = \begin{bmatrix} -1 \\ 2 \end{bmatrix} - \begin{bmatrix} 3 \\ 2 \end{bmatrix} = \begin{bmatrix} -4 \\ 0 \end{bmatrix}$$

(b)

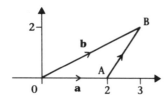

$$\overrightarrow{AB} = \begin{bmatrix} 3 \\ 2 \end{bmatrix} - \begin{bmatrix} 2 \\ 0 \end{bmatrix} = \begin{bmatrix} 1 \\ 2 \end{bmatrix}$$

(c)

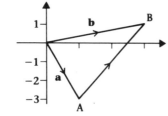

$$\overrightarrow{AB} = \begin{bmatrix} 3 \\ 1 \end{bmatrix} - \begin{bmatrix} 1 \\ -3 \end{bmatrix} = \begin{bmatrix} 2 \\ 4 \end{bmatrix}$$

(d)

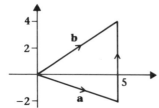

$$\overrightarrow{AB} = \begin{bmatrix} 5 \\ 4 \end{bmatrix} - \begin{bmatrix} 5 \\ -2 \end{bmatrix} = \begin{bmatrix} 0 \\ 6 \end{bmatrix}$$

2 $\overrightarrow{OP}$ represents the displacement from O to P.

$\overrightarrow{PQ}$ represents the displacement from P to Q.

The net effect is a displacement from O to Q.

$$\overrightarrow{PQ} = \overrightarrow{OQ} - \overrightarrow{OP} = \mathbf{q} - \mathbf{p}$$

3 (a) $\mathbf{c} = \frac{3}{2}\mathbf{a}$

$\mathbf{d} = 2\mathbf{b}$

$\mathbf{e} = \mathbf{b} - \mathbf{a}$ (Be careful: $\overrightarrow{OA}$ is of length 2 units!)

$\mathbf{f} = -\mathbf{b}$

(b) $\overrightarrow{AB} = \mathbf{b} - \mathbf{a}$

$\overrightarrow{CD} = \mathbf{d} - \mathbf{c} = 2\mathbf{b} - \frac{3}{2}\mathbf{a}$

$\overrightarrow{DE} = \mathbf{e} - \mathbf{d} = (\mathbf{b} - \mathbf{a}) - 2\mathbf{b} = -\mathbf{a} - \mathbf{b}$

$\overrightarrow{EF} = \mathbf{f} - \mathbf{e} = -\mathbf{b} - (\mathbf{b} - \mathbf{a}) = \mathbf{a} - 2\mathbf{b}$

$\overrightarrow{FC} = \mathbf{c} - \mathbf{f} = \frac{3}{2}\mathbf{a} + \mathbf{b}$

(c) $\overrightarrow{CD} + \overrightarrow{DE} + \overrightarrow{EF} + \overrightarrow{FC} = 2\mathbf{b} - \frac{3}{2}\mathbf{a} - \mathbf{a} - \mathbf{b} + \mathbf{a} - 2\mathbf{b} + \frac{3}{2}\mathbf{a} + \mathbf{b} = \mathbf{0}$

The sum of the vectors is zero because the net displacement around the quadrilateral CDEFC is zero. i.e. the vectors have returned to their starting point.

(d) $\overrightarrow{AD} = 2\mathbf{b} - \mathbf{a} = -\overrightarrow{EF}$

4 (a) Values of t generate the points as follows:

t	-3	-2	-1	0	1	2	3
$\begin{bmatrix} x \\ y \end{bmatrix}$	$\begin{bmatrix} -6 \\ -9 \end{bmatrix}$	$\begin{bmatrix} -4 \\ -6 \end{bmatrix}$	$\begin{bmatrix} -2 \\ -3 \end{bmatrix}$	$\begin{bmatrix} 0 \\ 0 \end{bmatrix}$	$\begin{bmatrix} 2 \\ 3 \end{bmatrix}$	$\begin{bmatrix} 4 \\ 6 \end{bmatrix}$	$\begin{bmatrix} 6 \\ 9 \end{bmatrix}$

giving the graph of the straight line.

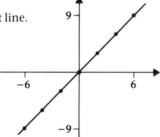

You can apply a similar method to (b) and (c) giving:

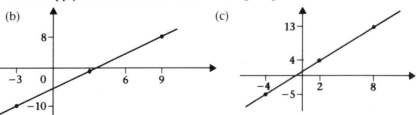

(b)

(c)

In each case the graph is a straight line.

The vector $\begin{bmatrix} 2 \\ 3 \end{bmatrix}$ gives the **direction** of the line.

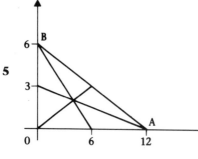

The three lines join each vertex to the mid-point of the opposite side. [Such a line is called a **median**.]

They intersect at the point $\begin{bmatrix} 4 \\ 2 \end{bmatrix}$.

6 (a) $\overrightarrow{OP} = \overrightarrow{OA} + \overrightarrow{AE} + \overrightarrow{EP}$ and $\overrightarrow{EP} = \frac{1}{2}\overrightarrow{EF}$

So $\overrightarrow{OP} = \begin{bmatrix} 6 \\ 0 \\ 0 \end{bmatrix} + \begin{bmatrix} 0 \\ 0 \\ 6 \end{bmatrix} + \begin{bmatrix} 0 \\ 3 \\ 0 \end{bmatrix} = \begin{bmatrix} 6 \\ 3 \\ 6 \end{bmatrix}$

Similarly $\overrightarrow{OQ} = \begin{bmatrix} 3 \\ 6 \\ 6 \end{bmatrix}$ and $\overrightarrow{OR} = \begin{bmatrix} 6 \\ 6 \\ 3 \end{bmatrix}$

(b) $\overrightarrow{PQ} = \mathbf{q} - \mathbf{p} = \begin{bmatrix} -3 \\ 3 \\ 0 \end{bmatrix}$ $\overrightarrow{QR} = \begin{bmatrix} 3 \\ 0 \\ -3 \end{bmatrix}$ $\overrightarrow{RP} = \begin{bmatrix} 0 \\ -3 \\ 3 \end{bmatrix}$

$\Rightarrow \overrightarrow{PQ} + \overrightarrow{QR} + \overrightarrow{RP} = \begin{bmatrix} -3 \\ 3 \\ 0 \end{bmatrix} + \begin{bmatrix} 3 \\ 0 \\ -3 \end{bmatrix} + \begin{bmatrix} 0 \\ -3 \\ 3 \end{bmatrix} = \begin{bmatrix} 0 \\ 0 \\ 0 \end{bmatrix}$

7E (a) $t = \dfrac{1}{2}(x - 3)$

(b) $y = -1 + 3 \times \dfrac{1}{2}(x - 3) \Rightarrow y = \dfrac{3}{2}x - \dfrac{11}{2}$

(c) The gradient is $\dfrac{3}{2}$. The vector $\begin{bmatrix} 2 \\ 3 \end{bmatrix}$ has gradient $\dfrac{3}{2}$.

8E (a) $x = 3 - 2s$ (b) $x = 1 + 2t$
  $y = -2 + s$ $y = -1 - t$
  $\Rightarrow y = -\dfrac{1}{2}x - \dfrac{1}{2}$ $y = -\dfrac{1}{2}x - \dfrac{1}{2}$

The two vector equations give the same straight line.

They have the same direction, $\begin{bmatrix} -2 \\ 1 \end{bmatrix}$ or $\begin{bmatrix} 2 \\ -1 \end{bmatrix}$ and appear to be different since different points on the line have been chosen.

Equations of lines

1 $\mathbf{d} = \begin{bmatrix} 4 \\ 6 \\ 0 \end{bmatrix}$ $\mathbf{e} = \begin{bmatrix} 0 \\ 6 \\ 3 \end{bmatrix}$ $\mathbf{f} = \begin{bmatrix} 4 \\ 0 \\ 3 \end{bmatrix}$ $\mathbf{g} = \begin{bmatrix} 4 \\ 6 \\ 3 \end{bmatrix}$

2 $\lambda = 0 \Rightarrow \begin{bmatrix} x \\ y \\ z \end{bmatrix} = \begin{bmatrix} 0 \\ 0 \\ 0 \end{bmatrix}$ $\lambda = 1 \Rightarrow \begin{bmatrix} x \\ y \\ z \end{bmatrix} = \begin{bmatrix} 4 \\ 6 \\ 0 \end{bmatrix}$

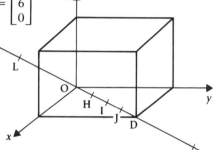

(a) So $\lambda = 0$ gives O, $\lambda = 1$ gives D.

(b) H, I, J, K, and L correspond to $\lambda = \frac{1}{4}, \frac{1}{2}, \frac{3}{4}$, 2 and -1 respectively. H, I and J are on the line between O and D.

(c) K and L are on the same line but outside OD.

3 (a) Since $\overrightarrow{OC} = \begin{bmatrix} 0 \\ 0 \\ 3 \end{bmatrix}$ the vector equation corresponds to the line OC.

(b) OE

(c) $\begin{bmatrix} x \\ y \\ z \end{bmatrix} = \lambda \begin{bmatrix} 0 \\ 6 \\ 0 \end{bmatrix}$ (d) $\begin{bmatrix} x \\ y \\ z \end{bmatrix} = \lambda \begin{bmatrix} 4 \\ 0 \\ 3 \end{bmatrix}$ (e) $\begin{bmatrix} x \\ y \\ z \end{bmatrix} = \lambda \begin{bmatrix} 4 \\ 6 \\ 3 \end{bmatrix}$

4 $\lambda = 0 \Rightarrow \begin{bmatrix} x \\ y \\ z \end{bmatrix} = \begin{bmatrix} 0 \\ 0 \\ 3 \end{bmatrix}$ i.e. point C

$\lambda = 1 \Rightarrow \begin{bmatrix} x \\ y \\ z \end{bmatrix} = \begin{bmatrix} 4 \\ 6 \\ 3 \end{bmatrix}$

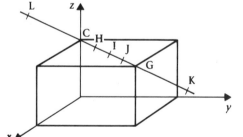

The points lie on the line CG.
H, I, J, K and L correspond to $\lambda = \frac{1}{4}, \frac{1}{2}, \frac{3}{4}$, 2 and -1 respectively.

5 (a) When $\lambda = 0$, $\begin{bmatrix} x \\ y \\ z \end{bmatrix} = \begin{bmatrix} 0 \\ 6 \\ 0 \end{bmatrix}$, i.e. point B. When $\lambda = 1$, $\begin{bmatrix} x \\ y \\ z \end{bmatrix} = \begin{bmatrix} 0 \\ 6 \\ 3 \end{bmatrix}$ i.e. point E.

Hence the line is BE.

(b) $\lambda = 0$ gives F, $\lambda = 1$ gives E, so the line is FE.
The two vectors each specify the **direction** of the line.

6 (a) The line AD passes through A and has direction $\overrightarrow{AD} = \begin{bmatrix} 0 \\ 6 \\ 0 \end{bmatrix}$

so it has equation $\begin{bmatrix} x \\ y \\ z \end{bmatrix} = \begin{bmatrix} 4 \\ 0 \\ 0 \end{bmatrix} + \lambda \begin{bmatrix} 0 \\ 6 \\ 0 \end{bmatrix}$.

(b) $\begin{bmatrix} x \\ y \\ z \end{bmatrix} = \begin{bmatrix} 4 \\ 0 \\ 0 \end{bmatrix} + \lambda \begin{bmatrix} 0 \\ 6 \\ 3 \end{bmatrix}$ (c) $\begin{bmatrix} x \\ y \\ z \end{bmatrix} = \begin{bmatrix} 4 \\ 0 \\ 0 \end{bmatrix} + \lambda \begin{bmatrix} -4 \\ 6 \\ 3 \end{bmatrix}$

NB. These are **not** unique equations. For example, AE also passes through E and

has equation $\begin{bmatrix} x \\ y \\ z \end{bmatrix} = \begin{bmatrix} 0 \\ 6 \\ 3 \end{bmatrix} + \mu \begin{bmatrix} 4 \\ -6 \\ -3 \end{bmatrix}$. Thus the point $\begin{bmatrix} -4 \\ 12 \\ 6 \end{bmatrix}$ is found either by starting

from A and putting $\lambda = 2$, or by starting from E and putting $\mu = -1$.

7 (a)

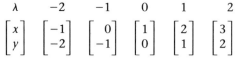

λ	-2	-1	0	1	2
$\begin{bmatrix} x \\ y \end{bmatrix}$	$\begin{bmatrix} -1 \\ -2 \end{bmatrix}$	$\begin{bmatrix} 0 \\ -1 \end{bmatrix}$	$\begin{bmatrix} 1 \\ 0 \end{bmatrix}$	$\begin{bmatrix} 2 \\ 1 \end{bmatrix}$	$\begin{bmatrix} 3 \\ 2 \end{bmatrix}$

μ	-2	-1	0	1	2
$\begin{bmatrix} x \\ y \end{bmatrix}$	$\begin{bmatrix} -3 \\ 5 \end{bmatrix}$	$\begin{bmatrix} -1 \\ 4 \end{bmatrix}$	$\begin{bmatrix} 1 \\ 3 \end{bmatrix}$	$\begin{bmatrix} 3 \\ 2 \end{bmatrix}$	$\begin{bmatrix} 5 \\ 1 \end{bmatrix}$

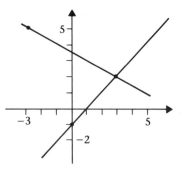

(b) The lines intersect at $\begin{bmatrix} 3 \\ 2 \end{bmatrix}$.   (c) $\lambda = 2$, $\mu = 1$ at the point of intersection.

(d) Since at the point of intersection both x and y coordinates are equal,

$$1 + \lambda = 1 + 2\mu \quad \text{and} \quad \lambda = 3 - \mu$$

(e) Solving these gives $\lambda = 2$, $\mu = 1$.

8 Equating the x and y coordinates,

$$2 + \lambda = 1 + 2\mu$$
$$2 + 2\lambda = 3 - \mu$$
$$\text{giving } \lambda = \tfrac{1}{5}, \quad \mu = \tfrac{3}{5}$$

Angles between vectors

1 (a)

Using Pythagoras' theorem, the length of **a** is
$$\sqrt{(3^2 + 2^2)} = \sqrt{13} \approx 3.606$$

Similarly, the length of **b** is $\sqrt{(1^2 + 4^2)} = \sqrt{17} \approx 4.123$

(b) $\mathbf{c} = \mathbf{b} - \mathbf{a} = \begin{bmatrix} -2 \\ 2 \end{bmatrix}$

So the length of **c** is $\sqrt{((-2)^2 + 2^2)} = \sqrt{8} \approx 2.828$

(c)

$$(\sqrt{8})^2 = (\sqrt{17})^2 + (\sqrt{13})^2 - 2\sqrt{17}\,\sqrt{13}\cos\theta$$
$$\Rightarrow \cos\theta = \frac{11}{\sqrt{221}} \approx 0.7399$$
$$\Rightarrow \theta = 42.3°$$

2 (a) As in question 1, by Pythagoras,
$$a = \sqrt{(a_1^2 + a_2^2)} \Rightarrow a^2 = a_1^2 + a_2^2$$
Similarly $b^2 = b_1^2 + b_2^2$

(b) $c^2 = (b_1 - a_1)^2 + (b_2 - a_2)^2$
$$= b_1^2 - 2a_1b_1 + a_1^2 + b_2^2 - 2a_2b_2 + a_2^2$$
$$= (a_1^2 + a_2^2) + (b_1^2 + b_2^2) - 2a_1b_1 - 2a_2b_2$$
$$= a^2 + b^2 - 2(a_1b_1 + a_2b_2)$$

(c) By the cosine rule,
$$c^2 = a^2 + b^2 - 2ab\cos\theta$$
So $a_1b_1 + a_2b_2 = ab\cos\theta$, since the two expressions are otherwise identical.

3 $\mathbf{a} = \begin{bmatrix} 3 \\ 2 \end{bmatrix}$ $\qquad$ $\mathbf{b} = \begin{bmatrix} -2 \\ 2 \end{bmatrix}$

$a_1 = 3, a_2 = 2$ $\qquad$ $b_1 = 1, b_2 = 4$
$a = \sqrt{(9 + 4)} = \sqrt{13}$ $\qquad$ $b = \sqrt{(1 + 16)} = \sqrt{17}$
$\Rightarrow 3 \times 1 + 2 \times 4 = \sqrt{13}\sqrt{17}\cos\theta$
$\Rightarrow \cos\theta = \dfrac{11}{\sqrt{221}} \approx 0.7399$
and $\theta = 42.3°$ as before

Scalar products

1 (a)

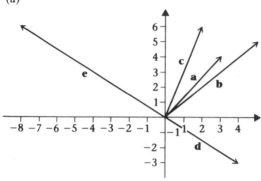

(b) **d** is parallel to **e**
    a is perpendicular to **d** and **e**

2 (a) $|a| = 5$, $|b| = \sqrt{50}$, $|c| = \sqrt{40}$, $|d| = 5$, $|e| = 10$

(b) **a** . **a** = 25   **b** . **b** = 50   **c** . **c** = 40   **d** . **d** = 25   **e** . **e** = 100

(c) **a** . **a** = $|a|^2$
    The scalar product of a vector with itself is equal to the square of its modulus.

3 (a) **a** . **b** = 3 × 5 + 4 × 5 = 35   **b** . **a** = 5 × 3 + 5 × 4 = 35

(b) **a** . **c** = 3 × 2 + 4 × 6 = 30   **c** . **a** = 2 × 3 + 6 × 4 = 30

(c) **a** . **b** = **b** . **a**   and   **a** . **c** = **c** . **a**
    You can conclude that scalar multiplication is **commutative** as a consequence
    of the commutativity of ordinary multiplication.

4 (a) **a** . **b** + **a** . **c** = 35 + 30 = 65

(b) $\mathbf{a} \cdot (\mathbf{b} + \mathbf{c}) = \begin{bmatrix} 3 \\ 4 \end{bmatrix} \cdot \begin{bmatrix} 7 \\ 11 \end{bmatrix} = 21 + 44 = 65$

(c) So, the **distributive law** appears to hold, i.e. **a** . **b** + **a** . **c** = **a** . (**b** + **c**). In fact,
    it can be shown that the distributive law holds for all vectors **a, b, c**.

5 (a) $\mathbf{a} \cdot \mathbf{b} = 35$, $\mathbf{a} \cdot \mathbf{d} = 0$, $\mathbf{a} \cdot \mathbf{e} = 0$

(b) If the vectors are perpendicular then their scalar product is zero.

(c) $\begin{bmatrix} -5 \\ 5 \end{bmatrix}$ is perpendicular to **b**.

(d) Since $\mathbf{a} \cdot \mathbf{b} = ab \cos \theta$, $\mathbf{a} \cdot \mathbf{b} = 0 \Rightarrow a = 0$ or $b = 0$ or $\cos \theta = 0$. Thus **either** the vectors are perpendicular, **or** one of the vectors is the zero vector.

6E

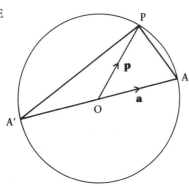

(a) $\overrightarrow{OA'} = -\overrightarrow{OA} = -a$

$\overrightarrow{AP} = \mathbf{p} - \mathbf{a}$

$\overrightarrow{A'P} = \mathbf{p} - \mathbf{a}' = \mathbf{p} + \mathbf{a}$

(b) $\overrightarrow{AP} \cdot \overrightarrow{A'P} = (\mathbf{p} - \mathbf{a}) \cdot (\mathbf{p} + \mathbf{a})$
$= p^2 - a^2$

But, since $|p| = |a|$, $p^2 - a^2 = 0$

(c) $\overrightarrow{AP}$ is perpendicular to $\overrightarrow{A'P}$
 . i.e. the angle in a semi-circle is a right angle.

Vector equations of planes

1

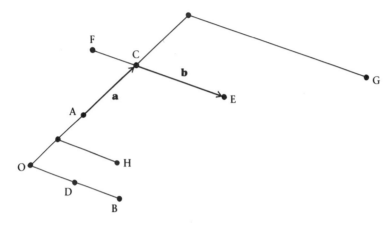

2 $c = 3a$ $d = 2b$ $e = -2b$ $f = -2b + a$
$g = 2a + 2b$ $h = 2b - 2a$ $i = \frac{1}{2}a + \frac{1}{2}b$

3 $\overrightarrow{DE} = \begin{bmatrix} 0 \\ 6 \\ 6 \end{bmatrix} - \begin{bmatrix} 6 \\ 6 \\ 0 \end{bmatrix} = \begin{bmatrix} -6 \\ 0 \\ 6 \end{bmatrix}$ $\overrightarrow{DF} = \begin{bmatrix} 6 \\ 0 \\ 6 \end{bmatrix} - \begin{bmatrix} 6 \\ 6 \\ 0 \end{bmatrix} = \begin{bmatrix} 0 \\ -6 \\ 6 \end{bmatrix}$

In order to reach any point in the plane DEF, it is necessary to go from O to D, followed by some combination of $\overrightarrow{DE}$ and $\overrightarrow{DF}$. Thus, if P is some point on the plane,

$$\overrightarrow{OP} = \overrightarrow{OD} + \overrightarrow{DP} = \overrightarrow{OD} + \lambda\,\overrightarrow{DE} + \mu\,\overrightarrow{DE} \text{ for some } \lambda_1 \text{ and } \mu$$

i.e. $\begin{bmatrix} x \\ y \\ z \end{bmatrix} = \begin{bmatrix} 6 \\ 6 \\ 0 \end{bmatrix} + \lambda \begin{bmatrix} -6 \\ 0 \\ 6 \end{bmatrix} + \mu \begin{bmatrix} 0 \\ -6 \\ 6 \end{bmatrix}$

4 The coordinates of each point are:

(a) $(6, 6, 0)$ i.e. D   (b) $(0, 6, 6)$ i.e. E   (c) $(6, 0, 6)$ i.e. F

(d) $(3, 3, 6)$ (e) $(4, 4, 4)$

5 The planes are parallel.

$\overrightarrow{CB} = \begin{bmatrix} 0 \\ 6 \\ -6 \end{bmatrix}$ $\overrightarrow{CA} = \begin{bmatrix} 6 \\ 0 \\ -6 \end{bmatrix}$

ABC has equation $\begin{bmatrix} x \\ y \\ z \end{bmatrix} = \begin{bmatrix} 0 \\ 0 \\ 6 \end{bmatrix} + \lambda \begin{bmatrix} 0 \\ 6 \\ -6 \end{bmatrix} + \mu \begin{bmatrix} 6 \\ 0 \\ -6 \end{bmatrix}$

6 (a) $(0, 0, 6)$ i.e. C   (b) $(0, 6, 0)$ i.e. B   (c) $(6, 0, 0)$ i.e. A

(d) $(3, 3, 0)$ (e) $(2, 2, 2)$

7 (a) If the plane is parallel to ABC then its direction will still be specified by vectors $\overrightarrow{CB}$ and $\overrightarrow{CA}$, but will pass through O instead of C.

The equation will therefore be:

$$\begin{bmatrix} x \\ y \\ z \end{bmatrix} = \begin{bmatrix} 0 \\ 0 \\ 0 \end{bmatrix} + \lambda \begin{bmatrix} 0 \\ 6 \\ -6 \end{bmatrix} + \mu \begin{bmatrix} 6 \\ 0 \\ -6 \end{bmatrix}$$

(b) Similarly the parallel plane through G will be:

$$\begin{bmatrix} x \\ y \\ z \end{bmatrix} = \begin{bmatrix} 6 \\ 6 \\ 6 \end{bmatrix} + \lambda \begin{bmatrix} 0 \\ 6 \\ -6 \end{bmatrix} + \mu \begin{bmatrix} 6 \\ 0 \\ -6 \end{bmatrix}$$

8 $\overrightarrow{OH}$ is $\begin{bmatrix} 3 \\ 0 \\ 6 \end{bmatrix}$ $\overrightarrow{HD}$ is $\begin{bmatrix} 3 \\ 6 \\ -6 \end{bmatrix}$ $\overrightarrow{HE}$ is $\begin{bmatrix} -3 \\ 6 \\ 0 \end{bmatrix}$

Plane DEH is $\begin{bmatrix} x \\ y \\ z \end{bmatrix} = \begin{bmatrix} 3 \\ 0 \\ 6 \end{bmatrix} + \lambda \begin{bmatrix} 3 \\ 6 \\ -6 \end{bmatrix} + \mu \begin{bmatrix} -3 \\ 6 \\ 0 \end{bmatrix}$

Cartesian equations of planes

1 $x = 6 - 6\lambda$ ①
   $y = 6 \qquad - 6\mu$ ②
   $z = \qquad 6\lambda + 6\mu$ ③

   ① + ② + ③ $\Rightarrow x + y + z = 12$

2 (a) A is $(6, 0, 0)$,   B is $(0, 6, 0)$,   C is $(0, 0, 6)$, which suggests that $x + y + z = 6$.
      $x = \qquad 6\mu$ ①
      $y = \qquad 6\lambda$ ②
      $z = 6 - 6\lambda - 6\mu$ ③

      ① + ② + ③ $\Rightarrow x + y + z = 6$

   (b) For the plane through O
      $x = \qquad 6\mu$
      $y = \qquad 6\lambda$
      $z = \qquad -6\lambda - 6\mu$
      $\Rightarrow x + y + z = 0$

      For the plane through G
      $x = 6 \qquad + 6\mu$
      $y = 6 + 6\lambda$
      $z = 6 - 6\lambda - 6\mu$
      $\Rightarrow x + y + z = 18$

3 $x = 6 - 6\lambda - 3\mu$ ①
   $y = 6 \qquad - 6\mu$ ②
   $z = \qquad 6\lambda + 6\mu$ ③

   ① + ③ $\Rightarrow x + z = 6 + 3\mu$ ④

   Eliminating μ between equations ② and ④,

   ② + 2 × ④ $\Rightarrow y + 2(x + z) = 6 - 6\mu + 2(6 + 3\mu)$
   $\qquad\qquad\Rightarrow 2x + y + 2z = 18$

4 Using the method of question 3,
   $x = 5 - 3\lambda + 2\mu$ ①
   $y = 2 \qquad + 3\mu$ ②
   $z = 4 - 6\lambda + \mu$ ③

   $2 \times ① - ③ \Rightarrow 2x - z = 6 + 3\mu$ ④

   ④ − ② $\Rightarrow 2x - y - z = 4$

5 $\begin{bmatrix} 1 \\ 1 \\ 1 \end{bmatrix}$ is perpendicular to the plane DEF. It is called the **normal** to the plane.

$$\begin{bmatrix} 1 \\ 1 \\ 1 \end{bmatrix} . \overrightarrow{DE} = \begin{bmatrix} 1 \\ 1 \\ 1 \end{bmatrix} . \begin{bmatrix} -6 \\ 0 \\ 6 \end{bmatrix} = 0$$

$$\begin{bmatrix} 1 \\ 1 \\ 1 \end{bmatrix} . \overrightarrow{DF} = \begin{bmatrix} 1 \\ 1 \\ 1 \end{bmatrix} . \begin{bmatrix} 0 \\ -6 \\ 6 \end{bmatrix} = 0$$

So $\begin{bmatrix} 1 \\ 1 \\ 1 \end{bmatrix}$ is perpendicular to $\overrightarrow{DE}$ and $\overrightarrow{DF}$, two vectors which lie in the plane.

6 $\begin{bmatrix} 2 \\ 1 \\ 2 \end{bmatrix}$ is also normal to the plane and the scalar products with $\overrightarrow{DE}$ and $\overrightarrow{DH}$ are zero.

Intersections

1 (a) (i) $\mathbf{r} = \begin{bmatrix} 0 \\ 2 \\ 5 \end{bmatrix} + \lambda \begin{bmatrix} 2 \\ 0 \\ -3 \end{bmatrix} + \mu \begin{bmatrix} -1 \\ -1 \\ 1 \end{bmatrix}$

(ii) $\mathbf{r} = \begin{bmatrix} 2 \\ 2 \\ 2 \end{bmatrix} + \lambda \begin{bmatrix} -3 \\ -1 \\ 4 \end{bmatrix} + \mu \begin{bmatrix} -2 \\ 0 \\ 3 \end{bmatrix}$

(b) (i) $x = \qquad 2\lambda - \mu \qquad$ ①

$y = 2 \qquad - \mu \qquad$ ②

$z = 5 - 3\lambda + \mu \qquad$ ③

Eliminating μ, ① + ③, $\qquad x + z \qquad = 5 - \lambda \qquad$ ④

② + ③, $\qquad y + z \qquad = 7 - 3\lambda \qquad$ ⑤

$3 \times$ ④ $-$ ⑤, $\qquad 3x - y + 2z = 8$

(ii) $x = 2 - 3\lambda - 2\mu \qquad$ ①

$y = 2 - \lambda \qquad$ ②

$z = 2 + 4\lambda + 3\mu \qquad$ ③

$3 \times$ ① $+ 2 \times$ ③, $\qquad 3x + 2z = 10 - \lambda \qquad$ ④

④ $-$ ②, $\qquad 3x - y + 2z = 8 \qquad$ as before

2 $3x - y + 2z = 8 \qquad$ ①

$x - 2y + z = 1 \qquad$ ②

If $x = 0$, $2 \times$ ① $-$ ②, $\qquad z = 5, \qquad y = 2$

If $y = 0$, ① $- 3 \times$ ②, $\qquad z = -5, \qquad x = 6$

so two points are A(0, 2, 5) and B(6, 0, −5).

(There are many others and many ways of finding just two points!)

Hence, a vector in the direction of the line of intersection is $\overrightarrow{AB} = \begin{bmatrix} 6 \\ -2 \\ -10 \end{bmatrix}$

and the equation of the line of intersection is $\begin{bmatrix} x \\ y \\ z \end{bmatrix} = \begin{bmatrix} 0 \\ 2 \\ 5 \end{bmatrix} + \lambda \begin{bmatrix} 6 \\ -2 \\ -10 \end{bmatrix}$.

3 At the point of intersection, the point (x, y, z) satisfies the equations of both the line and the plane.

i.e. $x = 3t$

$y = 2 - t$

$z = 5 - 5t$

So, $2x + 3y + z = 7 \Rightarrow 2(3t) + 3(2 - t) + 5 - 5t = 7$

$\Rightarrow \qquad t = 2$

Thus the point of intersection is (6, 0, −5).

4 $x - 2y + z = 9$ ①
    $x + y + 2z = 8$ ②
    $x - 3y - 3z = 2$ ③

②－① $\Rightarrow 3y + z = -1$ ④
①－③ $\Rightarrow y + 4z = 7$ ⑤
④$- 3 \times$⑤ $\Rightarrow z = 2,$
        $\Rightarrow y = -1$ and $x = 5$

Thus, the point of intersection is $(5, -1, 2)$.

5 $x - 2y + z = 1$ ①
    $3x - y + 2z = 8$ ②
    $4x - 3y + 3z = 5$ ③
    $2 \times$②$-$① $\Rightarrow 5x + 3z = 15$ ④
    $3 \times$②$-$③ $\Rightarrow 5x + 3z = 19$ ⑤

But equations ④ and ⑤ are inconsistent – it is not possible for $5x + 3z$ to be equal to 15 and 19 simultaneously.
Using the method of question 2, the line of intersection of ① and ③ is

$$\begin{bmatrix} x \\ y \\ z \end{bmatrix} = \begin{bmatrix} 2 \\ 0 \\ -1 \end{bmatrix} + \lambda \begin{bmatrix} -\frac{3}{5} \\ \frac{1}{5} \\ 1 \end{bmatrix}$$ (taking points $(2, 0, -1)$, $(\frac{7}{5}, \frac{1}{5}, 0)$ on the line)

and the intersection of ② and ③ is

$$\begin{bmatrix} x \\ y \\ z \end{bmatrix} = \begin{bmatrix} \frac{19}{5} \\ \frac{17}{5} \\ 0 \end{bmatrix} + \lambda \begin{bmatrix} -\frac{19}{5} \\ \frac{19}{15} \\ \frac{19}{3} \end{bmatrix}$$ (taking $(\frac{19}{5}, \frac{17}{5}, 0)$ and $(0, \frac{14}{3}, \frac{19}{3})$)

But, the direction vector of each line is $\begin{bmatrix} 3 \\ -1 \\ 5 \end{bmatrix}$

Thus, the 3 planes intersect in 3 parallel lines – a prism.
If the third equation is $4x - 3y + 3z = 9$,
$3 \times$②$-$③ $\Rightarrow 5x + 3z = 15$, which is the
same as ④ above.
In this case all three planes intersect in a single
straight line.

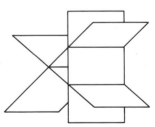

3 Binomials

3.1 Binomial expansions

> (a) Calculate 11^2, 11^3, 11^4.
>
> (b) What pattern do you notice?
>
> (c) What happens with 11^5?

(a) $11^2 = 121$, $11^3 = 1331$, $11^4 = 14641$

(b) 11^2, 11^3 and 11^4 can be arranged to give three successive rows of Pascal's triangle.

$$
\begin{array}{llllll}
11^2 & & 1 & 2 & 1 & \\
11^3 & 1 & 3 & 3 & 1 & \\
11^4 & 1 & 4 & 6 & 4 & 1
\end{array}
$$

(c) $11^5 = 161051$, whereas the fifth row of Pascal's triangle is
1 5 10 10 5 1. In this case the 10s have 'carried' into the next columns:

$$
\begin{aligned}
11^5 &= 100000 + 5 \times 10000 + 10 \times 1000 + 10 \times 100 \\
&\quad + 5 \times 10 + 1 \\
&= 100000 + 6 \times 10000 + 1 \times 1000 + 5 \times 10 + 1
\end{aligned}
$$

3.2 Binomial coefficients

> (a) What are $\binom{5}{0}$, $\binom{5}{3}$ and $\binom{5}{5}$?
>
> (b) Why does $\binom{8}{3} = \binom{8}{5}$?
>
> (c) Which other binomial coefficient is equal to $\binom{10}{2}$?
>
> (d) Why is it a sensible convention to count n and r from zero in Pascal's triangle?

(a) $\binom{5}{0} = 1$, $\binom{5}{3} = 10$, $\binom{5}{5} = 1$

(b) $\dbinom{8}{3} = \dbinom{8}{5}$ because of the symmetry of Pascal's triangle and because $\dbinom{8}{3}$ and $\dbinom{8}{5}$ are symmetrically placed on the eighth line of the triangle.

(c) $\dbinom{10}{2} = \dbinom{10}{8}$, by symmetry.

(d) It is sensible to link n to the power of the binomial expansion.

$$1$$

line number 1	$(a + b)^1$	1 1
line number 2	$(a + b)^2$	1 2 1
line number 3	$(a + b)^3$	1 3 3 1
line number 4	$(a + b)^4$	1 4 6 4 1

The top line therefore corresponds to $n = 0$.

Similarly, the first term in each row corresponds to the coefficient of $a^n b^0$ and is therefore the term corresponding to $r = 0$.

3.3 Binomial series

(a) Use the binomial theorem to show that the first four terms of the expansion of $(1 + x)^n$, for n a positive integer, are:

$$1 + nx + \frac{n(n - 1)}{2!}x^2 + \frac{n(n - 1)(n - 2)}{3!}x^3 + \ldots$$

(b) How many terms are there in the whole expansion?

(c) What is the last term?

(a) $(1 + x)^n = 1^n + \dbinom{n}{1}1^{n-1}x + \dbinom{n}{2}1^{n-2}x^2 + \dbinom{n}{3}1^{n-3}x^3 + \ldots$

$\qquad = 1 + \dfrac{n!}{1!\,(n-1)!}x + \dfrac{n!}{2!\,(n-2)!}x^2 + \dfrac{n!}{3!\,(n-3)!}x^3 + \ldots$

$\qquad = 1 + nx + \dfrac{n(n-1)}{2!}x^2 + \dfrac{n(n-1)(n-2)}{3!}x^3 + \ldots$

(b) $n + 1$

(c) x^n

3.4 Error and relative error

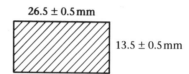

$6.5 \pm 0.5\,\text{mm}$

$3.5 \pm 0.5\,\text{mm}$

$26.5 \pm 0.5\,\text{mm}$

$13.5 \pm 0.5\,\text{mm}$

(a) What are the greatest and least possible values for

    (i) the perimeter   (ii) the area

of the rectangles shown?

(b) (i) Express the perimeter of each rectangle in the form $p \pm e$.

    (ii) Express the area of each rectangle in the form $a \pm e$.

(a) (i) Small rectangle : minimum perimeter $= 2(6 + 3)$ $= 18\,\text{mm}$
                       : maximum perimeter $= 2(7 + 4)$ $= 22\,\text{mm}$
       Large rectangle : minimum perimeter $= 2(26 + 13) = 78\,\text{mm}$
                       : maximum perimeter $= 2(27 + 14) = 82\,\text{mm}$

  (ii) Small rectangle : minimum area $= 6 \times 3$ $= 18\,\text{mm}^2$
                       : maximum area $= 7 \times 4$ $= 28\,\text{mm}^2$
       Large rectangle : minimum area $= 26 \times 13 = 338\,\text{mm}^2$
                       : maximum area $= 27 \times 14 = 378\,\text{mm}^2$

(b) (i) Small rectangle : perimeter $= 20 \pm 2\,\text{mm}$
       Large rectangle : perimeter $= 80 \pm 2\,\text{mm}$

  (ii) Small rectangle : area $= 23 \pm 5\,\text{mm}^2$
       Large rectangle : area $= 358 \pm 20\,\text{mm}^2$

Note that the perimeter is found by adding four numbers, each with an 'error' of 0.5 mm. The error in the perimeter is then found to be $4 \times 0.5 = 2\,\text{mm}$.

However, multiplying numbers with errors is not as straightforward. This is investigated further on tasksheet 4, where the idea of **relative error** is introduced.

Powers of $a + b$

1 $(a + b)^3 = (a + b)(a^2 + 2ab + b^2)$
$$= \quad a^3 + 2a^2b + ab^2$$
$$+ \quad a^2b + 2ab^2 + b^3$$
$$= \quad a^3 + 3a^2b + 3ab^2 + b^3$$

2 $(a + b)^4 = (a + b)(a + b)^3$
$$= (a + b)(a^3 + 3a^2b + 3ab^2 + b^3)$$
$$= a^4 + 4a^3b + 6a^2b^2 + 4ab^3 + b^4$$

3 (a) The coefficients form the rows of Pascal's triangle.

   (b) The next row is 1 4 6 4 1, as in the answer to question 2.

   (c) $(a + b)^5 = a^5 + 5a^4b + 10a^3b^2 + 10a^2b^3 + 5ab^4 + b^5$.

4E $a^4 + 4a^3(2b) + 6a^2(2b)^2 + 4a(2b)^3 + (2b)^4 = a^4 + 8a^3b + 24a^2b^2 + 32ab^3 + 16b^4$

NB. In Pascal's triangle, the sum of two adjacent numbers is always equal to the number below them:

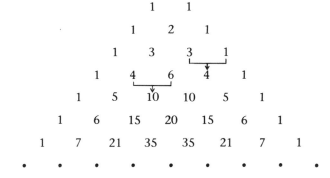

Binomial coefficients

1 The reciprocals of $\frac{4}{1}$ and $\frac{3}{2}$ are the factors $\frac{1}{4}$ and $\frac{2}{3}$.

2 (a) The multipliers for the 5th line are: $\quad \times \frac{5}{1} \quad\quad \times \frac{4}{2} \quad\quad \times \frac{3}{3} \quad\quad \times \frac{2}{4} \quad\quad \times \frac{1}{5}$

$$1 \longrightarrow 5 \longrightarrow 10 \longrightarrow 10 \longrightarrow 5 \longrightarrow 1$$

(b) The sequence of multipliers is $\frac{5}{1}, \frac{4}{2}, \frac{3}{3}, \frac{2}{4}, \frac{1}{5}$, where the numerators successively decrease by 1 and the denominators increase by 1.

3 (a) The multipliers for the 6th line are:

$$\times \frac{6}{1} \quad\quad \times \frac{5}{2} \quad\quad \times \frac{4}{3} \quad\quad \times \frac{3}{4} \quad\quad \times \frac{2}{5} \quad\quad \times \frac{1}{6}$$

$$1 \longrightarrow 6 \longrightarrow 15 \longrightarrow 20 \longrightarrow 15 \longrightarrow 6 \longrightarrow 1$$

(b) This agrees with the result from Pascal's triangle.

4 $\times \frac{10}{1} \quad \times \frac{9}{2} \quad \times \frac{8}{3} \quad \times \frac{7}{4} \quad \times \frac{6}{5} \quad \times \frac{5}{6} \quad \times \frac{4}{7} \quad \times \frac{3}{8} \quad \times \frac{2}{9} \quad \times \frac{1}{10}$

$$1 \longrightarrow 10 \longrightarrow 45 \longrightarrow 120 \longrightarrow 210 \longrightarrow 252 \longrightarrow 210 \longrightarrow 120 \longrightarrow 45 \longrightarrow 10 \longrightarrow 1$$

5E The sum is $1024 = 2^{10}$. The elements of the nth row of Pascal's triangle always sum to 2^n.

6 $\quad \times \frac{80}{1} \quad\quad \times \frac{79}{2} \quad\quad \times \frac{78}{3}$

$$1 \longrightarrow 80 \longrightarrow 3160 \longrightarrow 82\,160$$

7 $\dbinom{12}{5} = \dfrac{12 \times 11 \times 10 \times 9 \times 8}{1 \times 2 \times 3 \times 4 \times 5}$

8 (a) $\dfrac{12!}{7!} = \dfrac{12 \times 11 \times 10 \times 9 \times 8 \times 7 \times 6 \times 5 \times 4 \times 3 \times 2 \times 1}{7 \times 6 \times 5 \times 4 \times 3 \times 2 \times 1} = 12 \times 11 \times 10 \times 9 \times 8$

(b) $\dbinom{12}{5} = \dfrac{12 \times 11 \times 10 \times 9 \times 8}{1 \times 2 \times 3 \times 4 \times 5} = \dfrac{12 \times 11 \times 10 \times 9 \times 8}{5!} = \dfrac{12!}{5!\,7!}$ from (a)

(c) $\dbinom{12}{5} = 792$

9 $\quad \dbinom{12}{4} = \dfrac{12!}{4!\,8!}$ and $\dbinom{12}{8} = \dfrac{12!}{8!\,4!}$

$\quad \Rightarrow \dbinom{12}{8} = \dbinom{12}{4}$

10 (a) $\dbinom{12}{9} = \dfrac{12!}{9!\,3!} = \dfrac{12 \times 11 \times 10}{3 \times 2 \times 1} = 220$

(b) $\dbinom{12}{7} = \dfrac{12!}{5!\,7!} = \dfrac{12 \times 11 \times 10 \times 9 \times 8}{5 \times 4 \times 3 \times 2 \times 1} = 11 \times 9 \times 8 = 792$

(c) $\dbinom{12}{11} = \dfrac{12!}{11!\,1!} = \dfrac{12}{1} = 12$

11 $\quad \dbinom{n}{r} = \dfrac{n!}{r!\,(n-r)!}$

12 (a) $\dbinom{12}{0} = \dbinom{12}{12} = 1$

(b) $\dfrac{12!}{0!\,12!} = 1$

(c) $0! = 1$

Approximations

1 (b) $y = 1 + 3x$ is the tangent of $y = (1 + x)^3$ at $x = 0$, $y = 1$ and is a good approximation to the function near the origin.

(c)

x	0.05	0.1	0.15	0.2	0.25
$1 + 3x$	1.15	1.3	1.45	1.6	1.75
$(1 + x)^3$	1.157625	1.331	1.520875	1.728	1.953125

The results are close for small values of x but diverge as x increases.

2 (b)

x	0.05	0.1	0.15	0.2	0.25
$1 + 3x + 3x^2$	1.1575	1.33	1.5175	1.72	1.9375

$1 + 3x + 3x^2$ gives a better approximation than $1 + 3x$.

3 (a) $(1 + x)^8 = 1 + 8x + 28x^2 + \ldots$
so $1 + 8x + 28x^2$ is a quadratic approximation to $(1 + x)^8$.

(b) The approximation looks good for small positive and negative values of x. It is within about 10% of the correct value for $-0.1 < x < 0.17$.

4 (a) With $n = -1$, $1 + nx + \dfrac{n(n-1)}{2!} x^2$ becomes

$$1 + (-1)x + \frac{(-1)(-2)}{2!} x^2 = 1 - x + x^2$$

(b) For $-0.464 < x < 0.464$, the value of the quadratic is within 10% of the true value.

5 (a) $\sqrt{(1 + x)} = (1 + x)^{\frac{1}{2}}$

If $n = \frac{1}{2}$, the first three terms of the series are

$$1 + \frac{1}{2}x + \frac{(\frac{1}{2})(-\frac{1}{2})}{2!}x^2 = 1 + \frac{1}{2}x + \frac{(-\frac{1}{4})}{2}x^2$$
$$= 1 + \frac{1}{2}x - \frac{1}{8}x^2$$

(b) The value of $1 + \frac{1}{2}x - \frac{1}{8}x^2$ is within 10% of the value of $\sqrt{(1 + x)}$ for $-0.7 < x < 1.7$.

6 The next term in the series is $\dfrac{n(n - 1)(n - 2)}{3!}x^3$.

So, putting $n = \dfrac{1}{2}$ gives $\dfrac{\frac{1}{2}(-\frac{1}{2})(-\frac{3}{2})}{3!}x^3 = \dfrac{\frac{3}{8}}{6}x^3 = \dfrac{3}{48}x^3 = \dfrac{1}{16}x^3$

and a sensible cubic would be $1 + \dfrac{1}{2}x - \dfrac{1}{8}x^2 + \dfrac{1}{16}x^3$. This is a better

approximation than the quadratic, but is again good only for small values of x.

7E (a) The series is a geometric series, common ratio $-x$.

The sum is $\dfrac{1}{1 - (-x)} = \dfrac{1}{1 + x}$, provided $-1 < x < 1$.

(b) Substituting $n = -1$ gives $(1 + x)^{-1} = 1 - x + x^2 - x^3 + \ldots$, whose sum

is known to be $\dfrac{1}{1 + x}$ from (a).

If the binomial series is summed to infinity, then the series is **equal** to $(1 + x)^n$ for $-1 < x < 1$ and is not merely an approximation.

Relative error

1 $h = \dfrac{350 \pm 10}{14 \pm 0.5}$

$h_{max} = \dfrac{360}{13.5} \approx 26.67\,\text{mm}$

$h_{min} = \dfrac{340}{14.5} \approx 23.45\,\text{mm}$

$h = 25.06 \pm 1.61\,\text{mm}$

2 (a) $(1 + r)^2 = 1 + 2r + r^2 \approx 1 + 2r$, if r^2 can be ignored.

$\dfrac{1}{1 + r} = (1 + r)^{-1} = 1 - r + r^2 - r^3 + \ldots$

$\approx 1 - r$

(b) (i) $1 \pm 2 \times 0.05 = 1 \pm 0.1\,\text{m}^2$

(ii) $1 \pm 0.05\,\text{m}^{-1}$

3 (a) Maximum value: $(1 + r)(1 + s) = 1 + r + s + rs \approx 1 + (r + s)$
Minimum value: $(1 - r)(1 - s) = 1 - r - s + rs \approx 1 - (r + s)$
So $(1 \pm r)(1 \pm s) \approx 1 \pm (r + s)$

(b) Maximum value: $\dfrac{1 + r}{1 - s} \approx (1 + r)(1 + s) \approx 1 + (r + s)$

Minimum value: $\dfrac{1 - r}{1 + s} \approx (1 - r)(1 - s) \approx 1 - (r + s)$

So $\dfrac{1 \pm r}{1 \pm s} \approx 1 \pm (r + s)$

4 $h = \dfrac{350}{14} \times \dfrac{(1 \pm \frac{1}{35})}{(1 \pm \frac{1}{28})} \approx 25\left(1 \pm \left(\dfrac{1}{35} + \dfrac{1}{28}\right)\right)$

$\approx 25\left(1 \pm \dfrac{9}{140}\right)$

$\approx 25 \pm 1.61$

This compares well with the more accurate answer given in question 1.

4 The chain rule

4.1 Functions of functions

> A spherical balloon is being filled with air at a steady rate. How will the radius change as the balloon is being filled? Which of the graphs below is closest to what will happen and why?

The radius of the balloon will increase as it is filled. At first the radius will increase rapidly, but later the same increase in volume will give a smaller increase in the radius. The middle graph fits this description best.

4.2 Chain rule

> A rod with initial temperature 50°C is being heated so that its temperature increases by 2°C per minute. What is C, the temperature in degrees Celsius, after t minutes?
>
> To convert from degrees Celsius to degrees Fahrenheit, multiply by 1.8 and add on 32. Express F, the temperature in degrees Fahrenheit after t minutes, in terms of C and then in terms of t.
>
> What are $\dfrac{dF}{dt}, \dfrac{dF}{dC}$ and $\dfrac{dC}{dt}$? Can you find a connection between these rates of change? Think of other examples which involve two linear functions and see if there is a similar relationship.

$C = 50 + 2t$
$F = 32 + 1.8C$
$\Rightarrow F = 32 + 1.8(50 + 2t)$
$\quad F = 122 + 3.6t$

$$\frac{dF}{dt} = 3.6, \qquad \frac{dF}{dC} = 1.8, \qquad \frac{dC}{dt} = 2$$

$$\frac{dF}{dt} = \frac{dF}{dC} \times \frac{dC}{dt}$$

For all your examples you should find that the rate of change of the composite function is the product of the other two rates of change.

41

4.3 Differentiation by inspection

Can you see a way of using the chain rule without showing so much working? If so, try to explain what you do when differentiating $(4x + 3)^2$ and e^{3x} with respect to x.

$y = (4x + 3)^2$

$$\frac{dy}{dx} = 4 \times 2(4x + 3) = 8(4x + 3)$$

With respect to x, the derivative of $4x + 3$ is 4.

Think of $4x + 3$ as x. With respect to x, the derivative of x^2 is $2x$.

Similarly

$y = e^{3x}$

$$\frac{dy}{dx} = 3 \times e^{3x} = 3e^{3x}$$

With respect to x, the derivative of $3x$ is 3.

Think of $3x$ as x. With respect to x, the derivative of e^x is e^x.

4.4 Applications to integration

How can you find $\int_1^2 (5x - 3)^3 \, dx$?

$$y = (5x - 3)^4 \Rightarrow \frac{dy}{dx} = 4(5x - 3)^3 \times 5$$
$$= 20(5x - 3)^3$$

$$\Rightarrow \int_1^2 (5x - 3)^3 \, dx = \left[\frac{1}{20}(5x - 3)^4 \right]_1^2$$
$$= 119.25$$

4.5 Inverse functions and x^n

(a) If y is a function of x, explain why
$$\frac{dx}{dy} \times \frac{dy}{dx} = 1$$
$$\text{and} \frac{dx}{dy} = 1 \div \frac{dy}{dx}$$

(b) What connection is there between this result and the chain rule?

(a) For a locally straight curve:

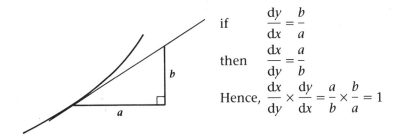

if $\quad \dfrac{dy}{dx} = \dfrac{b}{a}$

then $\quad \dfrac{dx}{dy} = \dfrac{a}{b}$

Hence, $\dfrac{dx}{dy} \times \dfrac{dy}{dx} = \dfrac{a}{b} \times \dfrac{b}{a} = 1$

(b) From the chain rule,
$$\frac{dy}{dy} = \frac{dy}{dx} \times \frac{dx}{dy}$$
However, $\dfrac{dy}{dy}$ is 1 and so
$$\frac{dy}{dx} \times \frac{dx}{dy} = 1 \;\Rightarrow\; \frac{dx}{dy} = 1 \div \frac{dy}{dx}$$

Multicubes

1 $z = y + 1,$ $y = \sqrt{x}$ $\Rightarrow z = \sqrt{x} + 1$
You should see:

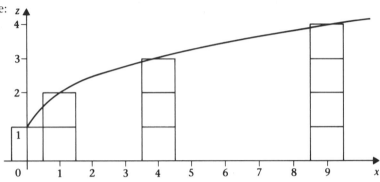

2 $y = \dfrac{1}{3}x, z = y^2$

$\Rightarrow z = \dfrac{x^2}{9}$

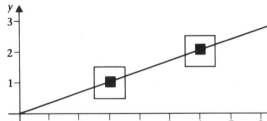

3 $y = x^2$
$z = 3y$
$\Rightarrow z = 3x^2$

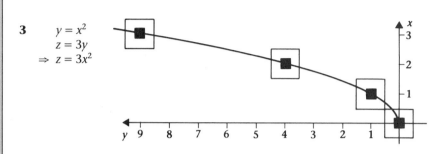

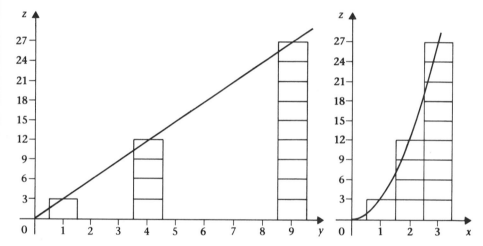

4

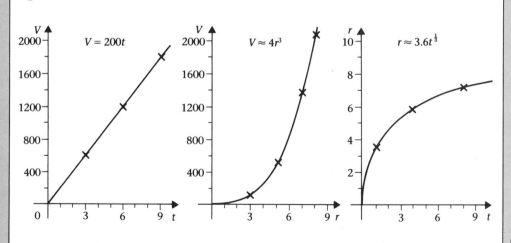

$V = 200t$

$V \approx 4r^3$

$r \approx 3.6t^{\frac{1}{3}}$

45

Checking the chain rule

1 (a) $\dfrac{dy}{du} = 3u^2$ and $\dfrac{du}{dx} = \cos x$

$\Rightarrow \dfrac{dy}{dx} = \dfrac{dy}{du} \times \dfrac{du}{dx}$

$\qquad = 3u^2 \times \cos x$

$\qquad = 3(\sin x)^2 \times \cos x$

$\qquad = 3 \sin^2 x \cos x$

(b) $y = e^{x^2}$

$\dfrac{dy}{dx} = \dfrac{dy}{du} \times \dfrac{du}{dx}$

$\qquad = e^u \times 2x$

$\qquad = e^{x^2} \times 2x$

$\qquad = 2xe^{x^2}$

(c) $y = (e^x)^2 = e^{2x}$

$\dfrac{dy}{dx} = \dfrac{dy}{du} \times \dfrac{du}{dx}$

$\qquad = 2u \times e^x$

$\qquad = 2e^x \times e^x$

$\qquad = 2e^{2x}$

2 The chain rule does in fact apply to any locally straight functions and you should have found that your results were confirmed by whatever numerical methods you tried.

5 Differential equations

5.1 Introduction

A murder victim was discovered by the police at 6:00 a.m. The body temperature of the victim was measured and found to be 25°C. A doctor arrived on the scene of the crime 30 minutes later and measured the body temperature again. It was found to be 22°C. The temperature of the room had remained constant at 15°C. The doctor, knowing normal body temperature to be 37°C, was able to estimate the time of death of the victim.

What would be your estimate for the time of death? What assumptions have you made?

The relevant data are:

Time (a.m.)		6:00	6:30
Temperature	37°C	25°C	22°C

You might assume that body temperature falls steadily. This fall would be 3°C in 30 minutes, or 0.1°C per minute. The body would then take 120 minutes to cool from 37°C to 25°C, giving the time of death as 4:00 a.m.

However, you know from experience that hot drinks cool rapidly to begin with, and then the rate of cooling slows down.

You could therefore expect the murder to have taken place well after 4:00 a.m, as the time of most rapid cooling would be just after death.

To make any further progress you need to relate the rate of cooling to other factors, such as room temperature. In particular, you can assume that Newton's law of cooling holds in this situation.

5.2 Algebraic solutions

Where possible write down the equation of the particular solution curve which passes through the point (0, 1) for each of the following differential equations.

(a) $\dfrac{dy}{dx} = 3x + 2$ (b) $\dfrac{dy}{dx} = 3x^2 - 2x - 1$

(c) $\dfrac{dy}{dx} = x \cos x$ (d) $\dfrac{dy}{dx} = x \cos x^2$

(e) $\dfrac{dy}{dx} = \cos x^2$ (f) $\dfrac{dy}{dx} = \dfrac{y + x}{y - x}$

Discuss why you are not able to solve all of the equations.

(a) $y = 1.5x^2 + 2x + 1$ This is easy to solve by inspection.

(b) $y = x^3 - x^2 - x + 1$ This is easy to solve by inspection.

(c) $y = x \sin x + \cos x$ It is far from easy to find this solution. A method is given in the unit *Calculus methods*.

(d) $y = \frac{1}{2} \sin x^2 + 1$ ·   This is solved by inspection using the chain rule.

(e) No solution   Although it looks straightforward this cannot be solve algebraically.

(f) No solution   The mixture of x's and y's complicate the search for a solution.

You have seen that even apparently simple functions cannot all be integrated algebraically. Areas under the graph of such a function can be evaluated by numerical methods such as the mid-ordinate or trapezium rules and these areas can be plotted to give the graph of the integral function even if it does not have a neat algebraic equation. In the case of (f), special techniques are needed because $\dfrac{dy}{dx}$ is given in terms of both x and y.

5.3 Direction diagrams

Complete the diagram for the second quadrant. What is represented by cooling curves in the second quadrant?

What would the third and fourth quadrants of this direction diagram represent? Complete these parts of the diagram.

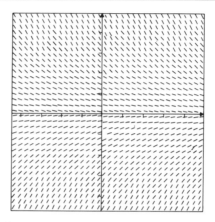

The second quadrant represents cooling curves before the (arbitrarily chosen) time $t = 0$.

In the third and fourth quadrants, the temperature difference, $y°C$, is negative and this difference gets smaller with time. These curves represent objects heating up, for example iced drinks.

5.5 Growth and decay

Check that you understand the analysis above. Generalise the argument to solve:

$$\frac{dy}{dx} = \lambda y$$

$$\frac{dy}{dx} = \lambda y \implies \frac{dx}{dy} = \frac{1}{\lambda y}$$

$$\implies x = \frac{1}{\lambda} \int \frac{1}{y} dy$$

$$\implies \lambda x = \ln y + c$$

$$\implies \lambda x + k = \ln y \qquad (k = -c)$$

$$\implies y = e^{\lambda x + k}$$

$$\implies y = e^{k} e^{\lambda x}$$

$$\implies y = A e^{\lambda x} \qquad (A = e^{k})$$

Cooling curves

1 (a)

Time	10	30	50	70	90
Temp. difference	53	29	16	9	5
Gradient	−1.6	−0.9	−0.5	−0.3	−0.1(5)

(b)

(c) The plotted points appear to lie on a straight line, i.e. there is a linear relationship.

(d) The gradient represents the rate at which the coffee is cooling.

(e) $\dfrac{dy}{dt}$

(f) $\dfrac{dy}{dt} = -ky$

2 (a) The time $t = 0$, at which measurements are first taken, can be chosen quite arbitrarily and need not be the same for all three cups.

(b) The gradients are all approximately -1.2, so appear to be the same for each curve.

(c) The gradients should all be the same (approximately).

(d) The gradient depends only on the temperature difference and is independent of the initial temperature.

(e) The curve which indicates an initial temperature difference of 70°C.

(f) $\dfrac{dy}{dt} = -ky$

Direction diagrams

1

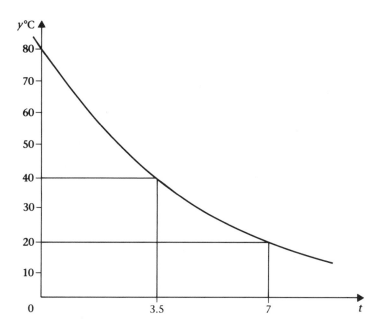

The curve shown above has been formed by joining together appropriate looking line-segments. Any such curve should give approximately the same results.

(a) 3.5 minutes

(b) 3.5 minutes

2 $\dfrac{dy}{dx} = x$

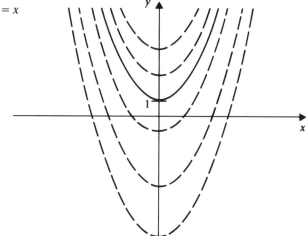

3 $\dfrac{dy}{dx} = -y$

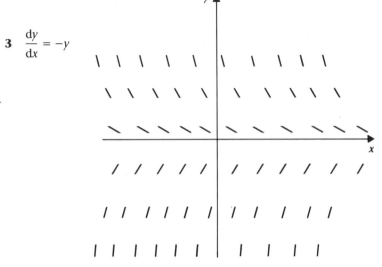

If y is initially negative, then y increases as x increases. However, y never becomes positive; it just gets closer to $y = 0$.

4 The direction diagram for $\dfrac{dy}{dx} = x - y$ is on the right.

(Note how $\dfrac{dy}{dx} = 0$ for all points with $y = x$.)

Solution curves for $\dfrac{dy}{dx} = x - y$

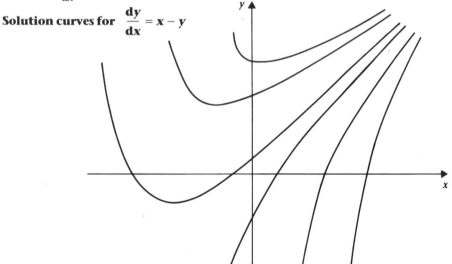

As x increases, y tends more and more to the value of x. (The line $y = x$ is an asymptote to each solution curve.)

5 The temperature falls 3°C in half an hour or 6°C per hour, which gives a time of death of 4:00 a.m., assuming the rate had remained constant.

The body is cooling from a temperature of 12°C above its surroundings, so you would expect Newton's law of cooling to hold.
i.e.,

$$\frac{dy}{dt} = -ky$$

You can estimate the constant k as follows:

The temperature drops by 3°C in half an hour. If you estimate $\frac{dy}{dt}$ to equal -6 when y is 10, then $-6 = -k \times 10$ and so $k = 0.6$.

$$\frac{dy}{dt} = -0.6y$$

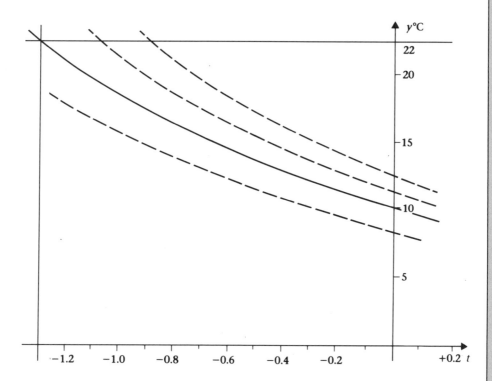

The approximate time of death is 1.3 hours before 6:00 a.m. or about 4:40 a.m.

53

Carbon dating

1   When $t = 5730$, $N = 0.5N_0$ and $N = N_0e^{-5730k}$

$\Rightarrow \quad 0.5 = e^{-5730k}$

$\Rightarrow \ln 0.5 = -5730k$

$\Rightarrow \quad k = 1.21 \times 10^{-4}$ (to 3 s.f.)

$\Rightarrow \quad k \approx \dfrac{1}{8300}$

2   $\dfrac{R(0)}{R(t)} = \dfrac{N_0e^0}{N_0e^{\frac{-t}{8300}}} \Rightarrow \dfrac{R(0)}{R(t)} = e^{\frac{t}{8300}}$

$\Rightarrow \ln\left(\dfrac{R(0)}{R(t)}\right) = \dfrac{t}{8300}$

$\Rightarrow \quad t = 8300 \ln\left(\dfrac{R(0)}{R(t)}\right)$

3   2700 BC is about 4700 years ago.
2550 BC is about 4550 years ago.

Assuming a radioactivity level of 6.68 when alive: $t = 8300 \ln\left(\dfrac{6.68}{3.8}\right)$

$= 4680$ years

This agrees with historical records.

4   4500 BC is about 6500 years ago.

Assuming an original radioactivity level of 6.68: $t = 8300 \ln\left(\dfrac{6.68}{2.8}\right)$

$= 7200$ years

There was strong evidence that the origins of agriculture were even earlier than at first thought.